A Man's Shield and Fortress

Stephen Ritchie

BookLeaf
Publishing

Presentation by *BookLeaf Publishing*

Web: www.bookleafpub.com

E-mail: info@bookleafpub.com

ISBN: 9789395271165

First edition 2022

Part 1: Set Sail on Adventure

Shipwrecked

She was a fine ship, a long time ago,
Vast white sails to catch either gale or breeze.
I had crew, but captained the ship solo.
I thought I'd sail the S. S. Success with ease.
She sported a beautiful mermaid bow,
And fine, flawless rigging all came with.
As far as guiding this vessel, only I knew how.
My pride was a sure, set monolith.
But I was blind to the holes carved in her sides,
And the tears forming in the once glorious sails.
When storms arose, my fear urged me to hide,
But the sea gives no shelter to one who bails.
I could not charter my own course any longer,
I prayed for redemption, a captain who was
stronger.

The hull of my life was a wreck,
But now I have an anchor to keep her in check,
And through storms, keeps the boat in place.
The carpenter is repairing this ship, by God's
grace.
The S.S. Redeemed is far more secure
Following one map to a celestial shore.

Healing hands have restored my keel,
And they now steer, as I hand over the wheel.

As I set sail for a mission and lands all new,
The sea still sends storms for me to fight
through.
Hurricanes and mounting waves peril my
charters,
But the Morning Star directs over these waters.
I will pull through these nights with more
endurance.
These monsoons can't shake my One Assurance.
It all makes the journey adventurous,
Inspiring themes for a sea shanty chorus.
All thanks to the god-man who walks on the
waves,
And who still stills the storms with His voice.
I would not trust anyone, but he who saves,
Despite the challenges, I would make no other
choice.
Let Spirit Wind fill my sails and be my guide,
Until I rest on the ocean's other side.

The hull of my life was a wreck,
But I always had an anchor to keep her in check,
And through storms, He kept the boat in place.
The carpenter refurbished a ship, by God's
grace.

The S.S. Redeemed is far more secure
Now having arrived at a celestial shore.
Healing hands have restored my heart.
Who had imagined those seas were only the
start?

Faith Frozen

Snow fall intensifies, and your view clouds
As the Winter Wizard guffaws aloud.
To keep faith frozen in fear is his goal.
This is the blinding, blizzard he deployed.
It was devised to steal, kill, and destroy.
It rages against the walls of your soul.

Death, defeat, dormancy
Are words he loves.
Life, joy, momentum
He loathes.
He believes his lies have triumphed.
But he did not anticipate the arrival of the Son.

Then the dawn delivers day, and the storm runs
out of steam.
Snowbanks soften into a new stream.
The mercury in the thermometer rises
Spring brings pleasant surprises,
Birds bounce on the breeze,
Bumble bees buzz
Ice glistens
Until
Gone.

The antagonist grimaces
In fright, against the blinding light.
The Son has dissolved all your fear.
Raise today your Ebenezer.
The revival of spring rebounds.
Your faith is no longer frozen
You are free, strengthened, and reborn,
And a new creation. Again.

Flowers blossom. They are just like
Newly finished masterpieces.
A deer laps from the fresh cascades.
A sprout is breaking through the earth.

Path Before Me

Trees cast shadows on the path before me.
The sun sinks as I glance over my shoulder,
 And I will not see the path clearly.

I press on through this grim realm of gnarled
trees,
I must get through. I shiver as it grows colder,
But I brave the path before me.

In bygone days I passed castles covered in
climbing ivy,
And danced through meadows dotted with white
clover.
On the mountains I could see the path clearly.

I could rest for the night to guarantee
I got sleep, and could gather food, look over
My supplies. Just postpone the path before me.

The trouble is I may start to feel too free,
Forget my path and let leisure take-over.
I must pass through the night though I can't see
clearly.

When my future is still a mystery,

My destination says there is good in store.
That is why I will walk the path before me,
Cause I will look back and see the path's
purpose clearly.

Adulting

Yes, I had some battle training
Sure, I have some simple armor
And a sword, but still, oh my word,
I didn't know I was being hemmed in,
Thrown in with the lions and warriors.
Everyday, life is so draining.

I'm here on the stadium grounds,
Having to fend, fight, for myself
No telling if I will win,
Or go down. The fighting's so hectic,
It's a coin toss, if my life's loss
Or I'll receive the victor's crown.

The whole crowd thinks I'm in my prime,
That with all my health and vigor,
Will always be invincible.
Who sees passed breastplate and visor,
To the face of a scared young boy?
Apparently, this is my time.

Heels of Disaster

You shudder at the roll of the thunder.
The lightning strikes tear the sky asunder.
The waves rise higher, you watch in wonder.
Soon the whole world is plunging down under.

You refuse rules or a master
Until you're left on the heels of disaster
When the sky is falling,
When the mountains sink into the sea,
Who do you have that you're calling?

The earth before you was split into two.
As you rose higher, the gaping gorge grew
Fiery comets in torrents raining down.
The mountain vomits lava over town.

You refuse a savior and a master
But as the winds spin faster
As the cold and warm fronts clash,
And the sky turns an ominous green
Where will you hide, to what will you cling?

What Childish Fantasy!

"Will you play with me?"
I look up from my book
To see the face of my little brother.
Young, innocent, excited eyes peer up at me.
Those were my eyes six and a half years ago.
I sigh,
I was almost done the chapter.
I have homework to do.
"I guess so."

"Yay!"
He hurries to our room
To get out the plastic castles and action figures.
I mark my place and trudge over.
I kneel on the floor
And wade through the sea of options
Of what childish fantasy
We are going to play.

Soon I am no longer a teenager
Playing pretend.
I am a sea captain fighting against
The worst storm I have ever seen
In my thirty years of sailing.
"Man over board!"

Cries my first mate.
I grit my teeth as I struggle at the wheel.

New kingdoms are created.
The king of my realm
Has just sent me on a mission
That every one of his best knights
Have never returned from.
I collect my sword from the blacksmith
And ready my steed.

"Dinner!" our mom calls.
"Coming!" replies my brother as he runs
Out of the room to jasmine rice.
I slowly stand.
I stare at our toy chest.
A treasure chest.
As I step forward,
My footsteps clop like horse hooves
And stormy gales ruffle my hair as
I adventure to dinner.

Pluviophile

I am a pluviophile.
I like sports and time outside,
Walks through the woods for a stroll.
But I love watching rain roll
Down the window from the inside,
Set with a book to confide.
Give me a sweet drink that warms,
I'm joyful during life's storms.

I am a pluviophile.
The part of me that loves Greek
Appreciates suffix, "phile".
The ending means, "One who loves".
To be Star Wars and LoTR geek
Means in battle and darkness,
You hold on to hope and light
In order to rise above.
To chain dragons and dark might,
I must train up ranks of knights.

I am a pluviophile.
God's my shield and my fortress
When I am found in distress.
I don't just live in denial,
I just trust Him through the trial.

He's working good all the while.
Sing praise and dance in the rain.
Celebrate despite the pain.

Part Two: The Tree Through the Seasons

The Seed

An acorn falls to the soft fresh earth,
A boy sitting with a teaching assistant,
Ready for sunlight and warmth,
Struggling to read words held up on flash cards.
First grade, they asked him why he had to go to
the back
For reading help.
A shoot is pushing through the ground,
Second grade, spelling was still hard,

And the teacher asked why paragraphs had such
big indents,
And why each page had such wide margins.
Roots are burrowing down.
Maybe some instinct in the child held the first
word back,
To build suspense,
Or left space on the page to dream and read
between the lines.
The first leaves are spreading up to the sky,
Third grade, he read well and enjoyed it.
He wrote, too, and his stories got "A's" and
happy face stickers.
Flowers are blooming like crimson dye.
Neither I nor they knew in college,
He would be reading the *Iliad*, conversing
Shakespeare,
The tree stands strong, ready to grow and bear
fruit.
Writing short stories and essays, and reading the
New Testament in Greek.
Birds perch and nest on every shoot.
Why didn't we though?
Acorns become towering oaks trees,
And mountain-moving faith sprouts from
mustards seeds.

Watering the Seed

Reading bedtime stories.
Ten Little Monkeys Jumping on the Bed
And *Ten Little Ladybugs* filled my head.
Guess How Much I Love You, *Love You Forever*,
And You and Me, Little Bear,
Filled the room with love and care.
Jamberry, *Berenstain Bears*, and Little Critter,
Gave us a laugh or two,
While *Goodnight Moon*, *The Little Engine That Could*,
You Are Special, and *Because I Love You*,
Helped to pull us through.

Orchard

I could never pick or consume them all,
But they're all beautiful where they are perched.
Their presence and crispness
In a joyous atmosphere manifest.
Kinds divided into different spaces,
You could walk up and down the rows for hours,
Your hands rubbing the wood
and fingers caressing the leaves.
I dream of a day when I grow this fruit,
But for now, I pluck my book
Off the shelf and devour it.

The Tree Still Stands

I stare at my screen, hand over my forehead
In pure frustration, after I have read
Three papers, for my three English classes.
Their marked critique from page to page flashes.
The feedback is all too true, and the grades,
Have left me swayed, no idea what to do.
The bare tree stood dormant after the fall,
Producing no leaves, taking in no light,
Yet it stood tall through every wintery squall,
Buried beneath a blanket of cold white.
Come spring, it remembered where it had its
roots.
Branches birthing fresh flowers and sweet fruit.
I am still a writer, and that's the way it'll be
Til the day, they take the axe to the tree.

The Secret to the Garden

To escape the chaos, I go to my secret garden,
A rich, green sanctuary watered by a spring.
The fountain flows out into a trickling stream,
I walk barefoot through the creek until I reach
the flourishing
Garden where I find all my fears and worries
dying,
And I sigh with relief that they no longer drown
me like a flood.

I drink in His presence from the spring until it
has flooded
My heart, and I lay on the soft grass, the carpet
of the garden.
This place restores my spirit when my soul is
dying.
Here flowers and trees are always in bloom like
spring,
And I pick and eat fresh fruit. I have a garden
where life is forever flourishing
That I want to protect, so I build a wall, not
caring if I block the stream.

So now when I leave, I walk a gulley once filled
by the stream,

And it might be a good thing; if it rained the
river could have flooded.
I hate leaving the garden when other places in
life are not usually flourishing,
And I often wish I could make the whole world
like the garden.
I know that's impossible because other places do
not have the spring,
So, I shrug and settle for the fact that elsewhere
plants are dying.

Yet when I return the next day my garden is
dying.
I scratch my head confused. I dammed the
stream
To keep as much water as possible from the
spring
From escaping. These drenched flowers and
disgruntled trees have a flood
Of water. I guess the spring is not all that the
garden
Needs, and I am missing what makes it flourish.
Then my old wish whispers to my soul how to
make it flourish.
The spring was meant to help the rest of the
world that is dying.
The spring was designed to flow out of the
garden,

But I foolishly robbed my neighbors by closing
in the stream.
Now my flowers are overwatered by a flood
That could flow out to the dry and thirsty
wastelands from the spring.

I run to the town to tell everyone on the street
about the spring.
At first, they don't believe any fountain can
make life flourish
Like I claim. That's when I go back, break down
the walls and a flood
Comes pouring out of my garden and the
landscapes that were dying
Begin growing new vegetation. The stream
Flows steadily again, and people begin to see the
source of hope for my garden.

The secret to the garden is it will start dying
If you fail to let the spring flow downstream.
Instead of making your garden flood, let it help
the rest of the world flourish.

Come and Go

Come and go
The glistening shells tumbling out with the tide.
Leaves fade red-dyed, fall and then glide.
This season,
We're friends separated by the distance
Had to choose something different.

New people
Make anxious over insecurities.
Wish to lock in place new loyalties.
But true friends,
Are magnetic. If they are authentic,
They will stick even through thin and thick.

Constant ones
The best ones, are shells you saved from the surf
And you keep in reach on your shelf.
When it's time
The leaves will grow back stronger too
Somewhat the same, but fresh and new.

Season Finale

We walk and talk and reminisce
About all our times together,
How the view has changed,
And everything I'll miss.
The sunsets over downtown.
The camera pans out
From the bench where we sat down.
"When Can I See You Again?"
By Owl City plays.
The credits roll.

The theme song plays
Over a new montage.
The sunrises on a new journey.
For a while, I was a tide going out,
Now I'm a tide coming in.
At the beach with new friends
Bouncing, bodysurfing the waves
Sea breeze, signaling the start of summer days.
All pruney, I gaze west as I emerge from the sea
And think of my friends drinking Turkish tea.

Part III: Flood and Flame

City of God

Finally found a place of peace,
Contentment in the chaos.
Though hate is hard
And strife is strong,
Here there is just joy and justice
And righteous reigns.
It took patience in pain,
But the king surely came.

The city is secure.
Watched over by wisdom
Walls fortified from fear.
The faithful stand strong forever.
Pearly gates, Paved gold
Roads rocking with praise.
Purified sinners
Parade in the streets.

The light of the lamb is loving.
The roar of the lion, The river lapping
The shores of salvation.
Zealous are the souls in Zion.
Agape at the angel choirs
Sighted over the crystal sea
The tree tells of the healing of the nations
Its leaves balm to the broken.

The poor are yet prosperous
Old riches only ruined.
Hearts healed, wounds sealed
Wonders revealed, rewards no longer concealed.
Every citizen created equal.
Grace fully gifted, mercy finally manifested.
This is where and when the righteous souls
Reaps what was sown.

Holy saints housed in the Holy city.
The feast fills the banquet hall,

The treasure troves bulk with the brave's haul
Rust won't rot splendor's spoils.
Destiny delivered, Divine decided to dine
Over morsels with mortals.

Crowns cast at the Father's feet.
Death's requiem rings dimmer
Along with the sealing of Satan's defeat.
Blessings blossom steadily
Sheathed in the Savior's brilliant beam
When you take a step of faith towards a dream,
The king will help it grow.
Dance in the River of Life's flow.

Interwoven

Strings of yarn, black, white, red, gold and
green.
They all have the same origin, fabricated in a
factory,
Yes, different colors, but spun from the same
kind of machine.

Intertwined they could tell by tapestry, a grand
story,
But for now, they are just individual threads,
spun out by one Fate,
measured by another, and then cut. A process
that is very orderly.

If they're just another string produced by
machine, they wait
Until they are measured and cut. They simply
lack purpose.
Unless someone saw their potential, believed
they could be something great.

So, what if instead they were handwoven by a
person?
A person who, because he made them, loved

Them enough to see their potential hidden below
the surface.

This weaver will have the strands become a
work worth talking of,
A tapestry forming a story in the picture.
What he weaves are creations undreamed of.

Interwoven into a single unit, like a chair of
wicker,
They could be connected like puzzle pieces,
Each string an element in a holy mixture.

Every thread, every color essential to his
masterpiece.
Until the end we will not see their collective
destiny;
But once this maker starts a work, it will not
cease.

Our lives are each a thread of tapestry,
We only ever see our string,
But in God's hands, he can weave us into
history.

Guardian of the Heart

My heart used to be known for its trading.
The city's gates opened to everything.
The gates welcomed the spoils gained by
raiding,
But also goods made by honest working.
As all the imports grew more illicit,
The evil of the exports grew more explicit.

Until the day a new king took the throne
He seized it by storm, to call it His home.
He is now changing my heart from the inside
out,
His forgiveness is my fortress devout.
Like strong walls, His love will never depart.
He stands as the guardian of my heart.

But I still bid forbidden goods enter,
Though I know they corrupt to my center.
I want to send vast armies out to fight
Whether or not the battles fought are right.
Why is this saved city still rebelling,
And wanting all this dark world is selling?

But if I bow to the king on his throne,
And the old ruler lies below tombstone,

This city will change from the outside in
It will no longer trade and deal in sin.
Each temptation will tremble at His Word,
Sin cannot enter passed a flaming sword.

Pencil Case

I open the lid of my pencil case.
As I grab my pen, the professor makes a face.
He comments on its untidiness.
I must agree; it is a mess.

Back at my dorm, I clean out the pencil case.
It's satisfying the remaining empty space.
I brush pencil shavings into my hand,
And they join broken crayons in the trash can.

Pencils with worn erasers get new tops,
And I dispose of pens whose ink has stopped.
Only what I need, all else erased,
Neatly laid out in my pencil case.

Better to be emptied of the old and broken, too,
Because from there you can be cleaned and
filled with the new.

Contrast

Tonight, gaze into the fire, an orange tent
Assembled from lighter fluid, matches,
Pizza boxes and some gathered branches.
It's the house where the heat and embers spent
The whole night dancing with some flitting
flames.
It was a roaring house party that raged
As long as oxygen remained engaged
In the action, unwilling to be tamed.
A fire should serve to illuminate where
There is a void, an absence of light.
A campfire is built to have warmth to share
During the times when it grows cold at night.
Be that comforting warmth to a world in
distress,
Be a beacon of light contrasting the darkness.

Lost Story

Talking over French fries
Trying to contain his dog Sky.
He's an artist and a convict.
I'm a writer and a Christian.
Speaking with me he retells the strife
And we're both striving to find
Our way through this crazy life.

For him, the world's so unforgiving
For me, I'm just yet to find it giving.
His parents divorced at five
The new stepmom didn't want him around
They put him up for foster care.
From home to home, just trying to survive
Once the ball kept rolling, it kept going down
To dream of breaking out, he wouldn't dare.

While the famous stories are told
Of millionaires with mansions
Who try to walk with a spiritual blindfold,
He sleeps under the stars.
Now he's laying bare his soul-deep scars.

While we worry and complain
About our apparent pain

We work and eat with no fear
And every day another outfit
Looks back at us in the mirror.

Despite it all, he cares for a dog,
He talks openly and smiles.
He rests knowing heaven's waiting
But I encourage and pray awhile
For Bill and his every worry.
For the man who told me his lost story.

Abandon Babel

I could build my way to the heavens,
Raise my tower to the sky.
Each minute, becoming every hour,
Create marvels to display my power.
I could secure every safe haven,
From the mast, fly my flag high.
I could even then become so incredible
The world believe I can do the impossible.
Until the tides of time wash it away
like a sand castle.
So I decide to today,
I will abandon Babel.

What good is it,
If God steps in to end it all?
Is it any benefit,
To gain the world, but lose my soul?
I simply waste my time,
If in the end, my kingdom falls,
At the last chime,
And the clock's final toll.

Leave Sodom and Gormorrah to disintegration
Let ash and sulfur be found by the next
generation.
No more building on the sand,

Only Christ the Cornerstone.
Construct what can't be built by hand.
A temple for the Spirit to call home.
From this foundation, it will weather flood and
flame.
The house may be humble.
The world may forget my name,
But I won't see it crumble,
If I obey the cross's call,
And choose to abandon all.

Then what good is it,
If I know only these three remain,
What benefit,
My soul as forfeit,
And the whole world as gain?
No reason to engrave my name,
Better to be a slave with no fame,
But know my heart is full.
To enter heaven, is the only goal.